D1636775

COMPLETE CAVALLETTI

COMPLETE CAVALLETTI

Basic to advanced training of horse and rider

PETER LICHTNER-HOYER

Translated from the German by
Jan Spauschus Johnson
for German Language Services

Publications, Inc.

COMPLETE CAVALLETTI is an approved translation of
CAVALLETTI-TRAINING by Peter Lichtner-Hoyer,
published by Albert Müller Verlag, AG, Rüschlikon-Zurich.

For information address:
Breakthrough Publications, Inc.
Ossining, New York 10562

Designed by Jaques Chazaud

ISBN: 0–914327–40–2
Library of Congress Catalog Card Number: 91–075122

Manufactured in the United States of America

Many thanks to all who helped me with
the work on this book:

The ladies—Jane Foxall, Christine Gerstmaier,
Jeschofnig, Eva Kasmader, Daniela Kramolin,
my wife Erika, and my daughter Katharina;
and the gentlemen—Helmut Feierfeil,
Volker Lerch, Andreas Puletz, Roland Springnagel,
and Werner Sramek.

Contents

Foreword by William Steinkraus   *ix*

1. Gentle Perfection: The Nature and
   Goal of Cavalletti Training   *1*

2. Preparation for Cavalletti Work   *7*
   Basic Requirements   *7*
   Length of the Training Session   *8*
   Equipment and Materials   *9*
   Setting up the Cavalletti   *15*
   Getting Started   *17*

3. Cavalletti Work at the Walk   *19*

4. Cavalletti Work at the Trot   *27*

5. Cavalletti Work at the Canter   *33*
   The Transition to Jumping   *36*
   A Word about In-and-Outs   *38*

6. Cavalletti Work in Traditional Riding
   Instruction and in Self-Instruction
   of Beginners   *41*
   Traditional Riding Instruction   *42*
   Self-Instruction of Beginners   *43*

7. Cavalletti Combinations at the Walk, Trot, and Canter 47

8. Cavalletti Work over Curved Lines 55
   Preparation 55
   Working at the Walk 59
   Working at the Trot 60
   Working over Alternating Curves 61

9. Cavalletti Work on the Longe Line 67

10. The Seamless Transition to Jumping Instruction 71
    Style Refinement 80

11. Cavalletti Work as Gymnastic Exercise for the Experienced Jumper before, during, and after Competition 83

12. Training Resumption and Gymnastic Exercising of the Convalescing Horse 89

13. Using Cavalletti to Lengthen Stride 95

14. Reschooling the High-Strung Horse 99

15. Reschooling the Lazy Horse 113

16. Reschooling the Sour Horse 117

17. Training the Green Horse 123

18. Design and Construction of Cavalletti 127

Index 133

Foreword

I am glad to have the chance to say a few words of introduction to the book by my old friend and riding colleague, Colonel Peter Lichtner-Hoyer, about the use of cavalletti in schooling horse and rider.

Peter and I entered the riding world (and with it "another world") at about the same time. We often met at jumper shows although we were both also interested in other riding disciplines and other sports. I am certain that what we learned from these other sports reinforced our belief in the value of rational, systematic, and constructive training in riding as well. This simply meant that over time we also came to appreciate the gymnastic value of cavalletti work in the area of our primary ambition—jumping.

From these other sports and activities—and they might be as different from riding as playing the violin is from playing golf—I also discovered a practical way to address technical problems: by breaking them down into their various component elements. I did not fully recognize the role that cavalletti could play in this mechanism until I met Bertalan de Nemethy, who had been trained at the Hungarian and German cavalry schools. Beralan de Nemethy was coach of the U.S. Jumping Team for twenty-five years, and under his leadership during that time I gained a clear idea of how to further the development not only of jumping but also of other disciplines through the gymnastic use of cavalletti. Peter was similarly influenced in his riding career, and a lifetime of experience gave him a chance to develop, revise, and shape a training method based on this. The following pages contain the essence of these reflections.

Naturally, it the end, it is always the horses that reveal to us the true quality of our work with them. The remarkable thing about Peter's riding career is not just his competitive success but the fact that his horses perform so consistently well and for so long. With this proof of success, the best recommendation for this book is its own content.

William Steinkraus

1

Gentle Perfection: The Nature and Goal of Cavalletti Training

After participating in the Olympic Games in Rome in 1960 I had the opportunity to study the so-called *sistema naturale,* the Natural Method of instruction, from the ground up and in its Italian homeland.* I was able to put all of its features to a practical test, as well as to study extensively the

Translator's note: The Natural Method, or Natural Riding, is the European adaptation of Caprilli's *sistema,* which in the United States is called "Forward Riding." *The Encyclopedia of the Horse,* ed. C. E. G. Hope (New York: Viking Press, 1973), p. 156.

basic premises of its brilliant founder, Federico Caprilli. My teachers and advisers during these years were two excellent Sardinian cavalry officers, Col. E. Chirico and Col. G. Cuneo. The knowledge and advice they shared with me, particularly about cavalletti training, became the basis of my later work, namely the development of a program of gymnastic exercise for the horse that uses cavalletti work to meet the challenges of today's equestrian sports. This is the program presented in this book.

Bertalan de Nemethy has always been a great model for me, not only because as a dedicated follower of Caprilli and coach of the U.S. Jumping Team he led his riders to such success, but also because that success was reached through a combination of performance and style that remains unequaled to this day.

It is common knowledge that the Caprilli method, with its basic principle of making corrections while moving freely forward, "sempre in avanti!," revolutionized riding. As early as 1910, for example, Oscar Caminneci, editor-in-chief of the German journal *St. Georg,* spoke out strongly in favor of adopting the forward seat for jumping. In the 1930s the Italian jumping style, albeit in modified form, was introduced at the cavalry's famous jumping academy in Hannover. In competition the forward seat was embraced so wholeheartedly that the approaches to jumps were ridden with no use of the seat whatsoever, leaving everything up to the horse and fate. Naturally this resulted in little real chance of success over uprights and combinations.

But, although the Italian School continued its overwhelming victory march across race tracks and jumper courses and into combined training, one of its special training methods fell into near oblivion and remains largely neglected today: gymnastic training over cavalletti. It is still used primarily as a tool in jumping work, even though, as this book will demonstrate, its areas of application and its advantages over many other training methods are so great that concentrated cavalletti work should be a part of the basic training of every horse and rider. Cavalletti work benefits not only high-level competition horses but also enables recreational riders, ambitious long-distance riders, and participants in the occasional low-level competition to improve the condition, agility, and above all the confidence and trust of their mounts.

There are, however, excellent riders and well-known trainers who acknowledge the advantages of cavalletti training but feel obliged to warn against "overrating" it. I hope that this book will change opinions like theirs. Naturally, cavalletti training, which is more than three-quarters of a century old, has required modification over the years. Even the Natural Method has changed over time, as already mentioned, and so, too, has cavalletti work.

I made mistakes during the course of my experimentation, and I certainly don't claim to have found the philosopher's stone. But I do believe that this carefully developed and tested method of cavalletti training offers the surest possible path to guaranteed success in reaching even the highest goals. This is based on the idea that the delayed sequence of movements that takes place when riding over a series of cavalletti at the walk and trot is a *slow-motion version of jumping.* Horse and rider face many challenges when jumping, in the approach to an obstacle, in flight, and during and after the landing. In slow motion, the training over multiple cavalletti presented here makes the rider aware of and drills the horse in everything that has to be done to overcome those challenges.

I believe that cavalletti work is the method of exercise that promises the most success and at the same time is the most considerate of the horse. The horse must lift its legs higher than usual, thereby strengthening the entire muscular structure. Cavalletti training demands increased concentration and accurate movement of the horse, thereby eliciting its cooperation and promoting its surefootedness. One important benefit of cavalletti work is the noticeable improvement in balance, in the ability of the horse under saddle to adjust its center of gravity to each new action demanded by the rider, and to carry out these actions, even during jumping or cross-country work, safely and without losing rhythm.

It is this aspect of cavalletti training that makes it especially valuable to that other participant in "Operation Cavalletti," namely the rider. Cavalletti work continually tests and improves the rider's ability to maintain balance and to bring the center of gravity in line with that of the horse. Thus, the rider is schooled in a primary task: to support the horse in the actions carried out, rather than to interfere with it, even inadvertently (the horse, of course, cannot tell a rider's intentional moves from the accidental ones). In this way, then, the ultimate goal of trust and harmony between horse and rider is reached. All of this is accomplished with the utmost consideration for the physical and psychological strength of the horse.

The importance of this point was impressed upon me throughout my long riding career. As most of that career took place in jumping I hope I may be allowed to make reference to that sport, although I would like to stress once again that the method of cavalletti training presented here is useful in the instruction of horses (and riders) in all equestrian sports.

At high-level competitions I had a chance to observe the styles and methods of the best riders in the world and to analyze their effectiveness. For example, I often spent long hours sitting in the exhibitors' stand at the CHIO [Concours Hippique International Officiel] in Aachen, watching with rapt attention the rounds of my colleagues from other countries. I have to admit that this intense immersion in my fellow competitors' performances demanded more of me than did my own rounds in between. In addition, I spent early mornings watching renowned riders and teams school their horses.

It became clear to me through these observations that the most successful horses were perfectly fit gymnastically, but during schooling were jumped only sparingly and over low fences—in short, considerately. In contrast, I was struck over the years by the incredible rate at which jumpers, particularly young and very talented ones, were used up. Herein, then, lies the answer to the question I am asked again and again in discussions with my students and with "believers" and "non-believers" alike: Why do I treat exercise with the help of cavalletti work as a central part of training? . . . Because it combines perfection with gentleness.

Today's horse is often mistreated, handled like a piece of sports equipment. The purpose of this book is not only to contribute toward helping each horse realize its full individual potential, but in employing humane methods while training it to do so.

2

Preparation
for Cavalletti Work

Basic Requirements

The minimum requirement for a young horse is
the usual training in the three basic gaits, with the
agility and responsiveness this normally demands.
It would be a mistake to start cavalletti work before
this stage has been reached.

Cavalletti work demands of the instructor, the
trainer, and the rider a logical program which takes
into account the level of ability of horse and rider,

as well as sensitivity and the ability to think for oneself. In cavalletti work there is no such thing as simply jumping on a horse and going off for an easy ride. Riders must become practiced at anticipating certain moves and must almost program those moves. It must become routine for them to make the right decision under time pressure and act immediately according to that decision.

An individual evaluation of the level of instruction of horse and rider is essential. Of course, it would be easiest to school intermediate riders on horses already familiar with cavalletti, but one is usually dealing with beginners and, even today, horses that are inexperienced in cavalletti work, so patience and a fine touch are required. Whenever possible, careful consideration should be given to the age and experience of the horse if the rider is inexperienced. In such cases in particular, of course, it would be ideal if a horse experienced at cavalletti work were available.

Length of the Training Session

The amount of training time devoted to cavalletti work also depends on similar factors. The young horse with little cavalletti experience should not immediately be schooled over them for an entire hour. It is up to the trainer or experienced rider to determine the appropriate length of each session; for example, ten minutes of warm-up work (which should always be done before any cavalletti schooling) followed by no more than about fifteen minutes of cavalletti training.

Exercise over cavalletti at the walk is especially important at this stage and should not be neglected, even if there is a certain monotony attached to it. In addition, it is important that with rare exceptions no more than four cavalletti in a row be used.

Equipment and Materials

The same saddle and bridle are used as in cross-country or jumping. Pay special attention to stirrup length. It is advisable to shorten the stirrups (the amount depends on the length of the rider's legs) to improve the rider's ability to maintain balance. Generally, the stirrup length is correct when the rider can stand in the stirrups and fit four fingers vertically between crotch and pommel (Fig. 1).

It is important to use a simple bridle, preferably with a thick snaffle, and naturally no auxiliary reins, although in some cases a loosely-adjusted running martingale may be used. In addition, at least the front legs of the horse should be protected in case they knock against the cavalletti. Simple

Figure 1. Shortening the stirrups: Length is correct when the rider can stand in the stirrups and fit four fingers between crotch and pommel.

boots that buckle or fasten with velcro offer suitable protection against superficial injury and help prevent splints (Fig. 2).

Either because they are unaware of the possible consequences, or because they lack time and the proper material, riders unfortunately often use normal jump poles when schooling (Fig. 3). Because these poles cannot be fixed in place on the ground they are extremely dangerous, especially for beginners. Cavalletti, with their crosses at either end, are stable, but poles roll away if knocked

Figure 2. Boots should be used to protect the horse's legs. (Unfortunately some photos in this book demonstrate that this precautionary measure is often neglected.)

Figure 3. Substituting normal jump poles for cavalletti is dangerous; they will roll away if knocked against.

Figure 4. Cavalletti with long, thin side pieces are also hazardous.

against. This can result in serious injury—including fractures—to the horse's legs.

The dimensions of a thoughtfully constructed cavalletti make it versatile and help reduce the risk of injury to horse and rider. Some riding establishments use cavalletti with very long—up to 24in (60cm)—side pieces, which stick up in the air and can cause life-threatening injury to riders as well (Fig. 4). How should a cavalletti look if it is to satisfy training and safety requirements for both horse

Figure 5. Upright cavalletti.

Figure 6. Half-height cavalletti.

and rider? A pole 10ft (3m) long and 3 1/2–4in (8–10cm) in diameter rests in the angle of a cross placed at either end of it. When the cavalletti is set upright, with the pole on top, the distance from the ground to the upper edge of the pole should be approximately 16in (40cm) (Fig. 5). When the cavalletti is placed on its side at half height, the distance should be about 10in (26cm) (Fig. 6), and when it is set low, with the pole on the ground, the distance should be about 5in (12cm). Directions for building cavalletti and the measurements of the individual pieces are given in Chapter 18, "Design and Construction of Cavalletti."

Cavalletti set at half height are the most useful for work at the walk, trot, and canter. The upright cavalletti is used primarily as a base for another set at half height (Fig. 7)—approximately 27in (68cm)—or upright (Fig. 8) on top of it, mostly for

Figure 7. Upright with half-height on top.

Figure 8. Upright with upright on top.

Figure 9. Typical combination of trot and canter cavalletti plus jump (here a post and rails).

cavalletti combinations at the canter. The more advanced the level of training the more combinations are possible, including some with the usual uprights and oxers (Fig. 9).

Setting up the Cavalletti

It is very important to know how much space there should be between walk, trot, and canter cavalletti. The intervals should measure:

— 5 to 5 1/2 ft (1.5–1.6m) for walk cavalletti (the horse should set each foot down once in between each cavalletti),

— 4 to 4 1/2 ft (1.3–1.4m) for trot cavalletti,

— approximately 20 ft (6m) or about 6 long human paces* for canter cavalletti.

Never let anyone convince you to use shorter

* *Translator's note:* "Paces" will be used throughout the book to refer to human strides, as opposed to strides of the horse.

Figure 10. A row of walk cavalletti.

distances that force the horse to place a foot in a new cavalletti space with each step. Young horses cannot be asked to maintain rhythm and balance while supporting the rider's weight if the intervals between cavalletti are so small that they have no chance to make corrections. This is why walk cavalletti should be set up at the aforementioned interval of 5 to 5 1/2 ft (1.5–1.6m) (Fig. 10). This allows the horse a step in between and provides the opportunity required for corrections.

It sometimes seems necessary to remind ourselves that the horse has *four* legs. Above all, the prescribed distances prevent injuries caused by the horse hitting its legs against the poles. They also support the horse psychologically by providing it with better information and building its trust. For the less able horse, the difficulty of separating even four cavalletti placed too closely together can result in leg injuries and a damaged sense of trust in the rider. This results in a frustrated and sour horse.

Getting Started

Once the proper equipment has been assembled, the work of familiarizing horse and rider with the cavalletti can begin.

Horse and rider should get used to the shorter stirrup length at all three basic gaits. Then halts should be practiced at the walk and trot, with emphasis on coordinated use of aids, in the following order:

— increased leg pressure,

— a straightening of the upper body,

— a deep forward-driving seat,

— the introduction of quarter halts,

— and all of this despite shortened stirrups.

When performing halts at the walk and trot, the hands should give elastically. As speed is reduced, the forward-driving pressure of the leg collects the horse's hindquarters under it.

3

Cavalletti Work at the Walk

As a first introduction, the horse, warmed up and on the bit, should be ridden over a low cavalletti. The rider maintains a straight upper body, but moves with the horse more than is usual at the walk. From three to six paces in front of the cavalletti (more about this "point of position" in a moment) to about three paces past it the rider supports the horse with a flexible, giving hand. Talking calmly to the horse is also recommended, as it builds trust and helps make the execution of this first exercise as calm and fluid as possible. Once over the cavalletti the reins are collected again and rhythm is reestablished if necessary.

While trot cavalletti are the most frequently used in schooling and can be ridden in the greatest variety of ways, the responsible trainer and rider will begin with walk cavalletti. Real training is thus begun by walking over two low cavalletti, which, as mentioned before, are set a distance of 5 to 5 1/2 ft (1.5–1.6m) apart. Only when the horse does this willingly and satisfactorily and the balance between horse and rider has been established should work over a row of four low cavalletti be tackled. Later the cavalletti will be raised to half height.

Even over this formation a wide range of styles can be observed, ranging from a deep seat aimed at achieving collection to extremely intrusive use of the hands. What is correct?

The horse should be ridden on the bit and at a normal walk and in normal carriage toward the middle of the first cavalletti, up to the point of position about three to six paces in front of the obstacle. At this distance from the cavalletti the rider should straighten the upper body and push forward with the back and seat muscles, thereby moving the horse on and bringing its hindquarters under it (Fig. 11).

This intensified forward-moving support helps the horse find the proper point at which to step

Figure 11. Use of the seat is increased from the point of position.

over the first cavalletti (Fig. 12). This, then, is where the central theme of the Italian system, correcting while moving freely forward, comes into play. The horse should never be forced into absolute obedience, so to speak, by sharp jerks of the reins or exaggerated halts.

Starting at the point of position and coordinated with the increased use of the back muscles, the rider's hands should give a maximum of two to four inches in the direction of the horse's mouth. Here the difficulty for the rider lies in giving with the hands while maintaining the forward push of the back and seat. Always make sure that the rider with little cavalletti experience maintains a straight upper body, at least until the first cavalletti is reached.

As the horse negotiates the first cavalletti the

Figure 12. The horse finds the proper point at which to step over the first cavalletti.

rider releases the hands further in the direction of the horse's mouth and at the same time goes into a suspended seat. This is basically a more controlled light seat that ensures an absolutely correct coordination of the center of gravity of both horse and rider.* With this, a phase of suspension begins that lasts until the last cavalletti has been negotiated. In

Translator's note: "The light seat is a light-sitting seat, somewhere between the forward jumping seat and the dressage seat. It is used between fences—often on the approach to a fence—and with short stirrups when working a jumping horse on the flat." *Advanced Techniques of Riding: The Official Instruction Handbook of the German National Equestrian Federation.* (Gaithersburg, MD: Half Halt Press, 1987), pp. 89–90.

Figure 13. The phase of suspension begins.

the suspended phase the rider must stay balanced while the horse finds the right rhythm. The rider encourages the horse by using the suspended seat and releasing the reins, allowing it the freedom to extend its neck and round its back and step rhythmically over the cavalletti (Fig. 13). Only after the last cavalletti does the rider sit down gently in the saddle, straighten up, and begin to control the pace of the horse and to restore timing and rhythm.

The series of movements performed over a row of walk cavalletti as described here gives both horse and rider a chance to prepare for each move in a calm and timely manner, to "program" the moves, and to carry them out quietly and promptly as well. Cavalletti work at the walk has the advantage of letting the horse and rider utilize the slow-motion effect, although the lack of forward impulsion at this slow pace causes problems for the rider in particular, as the task of maintaining balance with a constantly shifting center of gravity is difficult.

Certainly, compared to trot and canter cavalletti, walk cavalletti are not exactly exciting, but I cannot stress often enough the effectiveness of this work. The horse's muscles, tendons, and ligaments benefit from the unique gymnastic exercise and increased circulation. The calm, slow first stage of cavalletti work benefits the horse psychologically as well, making it more even-tempered and better able to handle stress. The row of four walk cavalletti can later be extended to a series of eight to twelve, further promoting consistent and pure timing and rhythm of the horse's stride. A series of this many cavalletti should be used only very sporadically, however.

Figure 14. Removing one out of a row of walk cavalletti.

I also recommend the practice of removing one out of a long row of cavalletti (Fig. 14). The resulting interval should be ridden in such a manner that the cavalletti following it can be negotiated without a change in rhythm. Another variation of the extended row of walk cavalletti can be used to evaluate the level of confidence and trust of the horse as well as the ability of the rider. Back when I was in Sardinia and had somewhat mastered the walk cavalletti—at least to the satisfaction of my Italian instructor—he went down a row of properly spaced cavalletti and shoved them out of place, shifting them arbitrarily and irregularly. Then he told me to ride through them in the manner I had learned. To my amazement the horse—on as long

Figure 15. Walk cavalletti at irregular intervals.

a rein as possible, I must emphasize—went through the cavalletti with absolute confidence and without a trace of anxiety, and without making a single mistake (Fig. 15). Freeing the neck by releasing the reins allows it to function as a balancing rod, which helps solve the problem.

Additional challenges are posed by walk cavalletti formations over curved lines. We will discuss these in Chapter 8.

4

Cavalletti Work
at the Trot

Horse and rider earn their spurs, so to speak, in training over cavalletti at the walk. The fundamental experience gained there proves valuable in work at the trot, which is performed at first over only a few cavalletti. A new experience for both rider and horse, and one they will notice right away, is that the impulsion and forward motion of the trot are an enormous help in cavalletti work. They make it much less difficult for horse and rider to find and keep their balance; for the rider, the important task

Figure 16. Point of position before a row of trot cavalletti.

of maintaining the correct seat with respect to the center of gravity is considerably easier.

At the beginning of trot work two to three low cavalletti are set up not too far apart—at intervals of about 4ft (1.3m), as specified earlier. They should be approached at a quiet rising trot. Following a few strides at a sitting trot, the rider reaches the point of position (Fig. 16). Here the rider starts to use the seat and hands to control tempo and timing so that the horse trots calmly up to the cavalletti. At the same time the rider must release the hands in the direction of the horse's mouth, so that more of the initiative of maintaining balance is transferred to the horse. The rider's torso remains upright, and the increased use of the seat supports the last trotting strides up to the first cavalletti. This is crucial if the horse is to find the right take-off point for the first cavalletti.

As the horse goes over the first cavalletti the rider extends the hands further in the direction of the horse's mouth and moves the upper body forward and up, introducing the phase of suspension and maintaining the suspended seat over all the cavalletti. After the last cavalletti the rider sinks gently into the saddle, straightens the torso and collects the reins, and reestablishes rhythm and timing at the sitting trot before moving on at a rising trot. In principle everything is done the way it was over walk cavalletti, except that the slow-motion effect is more obvious than at the normal trot tempo.

As noted, in the beginning two or perhaps three low cavalletti are used to gain the confidence required to negotiate successfully four half-height cavalletti with cadence in the next phase of practice (Fig. 17).

In order to state again more precisely the sig-

Figure 17. Trotting with cadence over a row of cavalletti.

nificance of the cavalletti work presented up to this point, we need to return to the slow-motion effect already mentioned, as well as to skip ahead to the subject of jumping training.

The method of walk and trot cavalletti work presented here is founded among other things on one of the most important insights provided by my many years of practical experience in cavalletti training: that *this variation of cavalletti work duplicates exactly the sequence of movements that takes place when jumping an obstacle.* In other words, the actions performed by horse and rider during the approach to a jump, at the take-off, in flight, and upon landing are all present—in a slower version and in slow motion—when walking or trotting over four cavalletti. These actions are slowed the most over walk cavalletti and are somewhat faster over trot cavalletti. This basic premise runs like a thread through the entire training program and determines the structure of all of the exercises.

The successful negotiation of a single jump takes place in the following stages: The rider approaches an upright (the height does not matter at this point), controlling the horse's canter by use of the seat and if necessary sustained rein aids, and exerting a gentle but increasingly firm influence over the horse. As soon as the point of position is reached, the rider intensifies the use of the forward-driving seat aids. By straightening the upper body the rider emphasizes the last two or three canter strides in such a way that the forward push of the seat is strongest on the final stride, helping to determine the best possible take-off point and aiding the horse over the approach so that it finds that point.

Over the jump, the rider moves actively in co-ordination with the horse's movements. Through the emphasis on forward motion—a properly balanced forward seat, and hands that give elastically without interfering—the rider gives the horse the necessary freedom to round the back, as well as the freedom to use head and neck to stretch out as far as possible and maintain balance.

Upon landing, the rider begins to regulate the tempo again by gently sitting back down in the saddle and retaining a balanced seat while straightening the torso and collecting the reins.

This, then, is the detailed sequence of actions that takes place when jumping an obstacle. If I compare this to the series of movements that takes place when riding over walk or trot cavalletti, I can easily recognize the slow-motion effect: The parabola of the single jump goes from take-off over a vertex to the landing, and this culmination point is multiplied by four over a row of four walk or trot cavalletti, with the series of movements carried out at a reduced speed (Fig. 18).

This results in training possibilities that offer

the advantages outlined—clearly, I hope—above, advantages that until now were unavailable: a high degree of gymnastic exercise even at the walk and trot, combined with very gentle physical and psychological treatment of the horse. The following chapters illustrate how these advantages stand up to more demanding work: The gymnastic exercise reaches its highest possible level but retains a considerateness for the horse that is rare in conventional training. And don't forget that at the same time the rider is taught to maintain balance and equilibrium.

Figure 18. Freeing the horse's back over trot cavalletti.

5

Cavalletti Work
at the Canter

In principle, the sequence of movements described in detail in the previous chapter is repeated in cavalletti work at the canter. The primary difference lies in the faster tempo and the increased impulsion it provides. The tempo of the canter works to advantage on the one hand, facilitating the maintenance of a balanced seat and of equilibrium between horse and rider. On the other hand, it demands much swifter reactions and results.

As a general rule I begin the cavalletti forma-

Figure 19. Higher version of the simple canter cavalletti combination; distance 6 paces.

tion for training at the canter with a cavalletti set at half height, which I call the canter-distance cavalletti. This is followed by a space of six long paces (approximately 20ft/6m) and an upright cavalletti. For an easier combination, the canter-distance cavalletti is set low and is followed by a space of six and a half paces and the upright cavalletti with a low cavalletti set directly in front of it to provide a ground line.

Figure 19 shows a somewhat higher version of this simple canter cavalletti combination: The canter-distance cavalletti is set at half height and is followed by a space of six paces and an upright cavalletti with another set at half height on top of it. In the beginning, these more challenging combinations should be practiced down the long side of a ring or arena, so that horse and rider have a visible boundary.

Sitting at the canter, the rider should guide the horse in a calm, controlled manner as much toward

Figure 20. Correct position of the rider over the canter-distance cavalletti.

the middle of the cavalletti as possible. Once again, starting at the point of position the rider increases support of the last two or three strides through use of the seat, at the same time moving the hands a bit in the direction of the horse's mouth. The rider— and this requires a deliberate effort—continues over the canter-distance cavalletti in the same way, with an erect upper body and driving seat, if necessary releasing the reins a bit more but maintaining an upright torso (Fig. 20). This deliberate negotiation of the canter-distance cavalletti is followed by one canter stride and then the jump over the upright and half-height cavalletti arrangement.

Special emphasis should be placed on the elastic release of the rider's hands forward and downward, in the direction of the horse's mouth. The hands should never remain fixed or move backward. The rider should learn early on to open the fingers if coordination of balance with the horse is ever lost. That way the reins will slide through the fingers and the rider will avoid abusing the horse's mouth through rigid use of the reins. It is better that the novice learn to jump with reins that are too long; once the rider knows how to overcome these difficulties it will be easier to return to using an economical release of the reins.

Thus the rider learns to ride the last two canter strides before the jump in a controlled and supportive manner, and the responsiveness and agility of the horse improve, ensuring a seamless transition to jumping.

The Transition to Jumping

A further intensification of cavalletti training, in which two upright cavalletti are placed one on top of the other and in which one additional low cavalletti may be used, can really be considered actual jumping training (Fig. 21), for which cavalletti work at the canter is definitely the preparatory link.

The confidence horse and rider gain from cavalletti training at the canter will later enable them to overcome cross-country jumps and single obstacles without approach aids, as well as to successfully negotiate combinations on a jumper course in a self-determined rhythm (not one dic-

Figure 21. Transition to jumping with the help of a canter-distance cavalletti (canter-distance cavalletti at half height/ space of 6 paces/jump of 2 upright and 1 low cavalletti).

tated by the cavalletti). Herein lies the difference between canter cavalletti on the one hand and single fences and combinations on the other; most importantly, the spaces between the canter caval-letti help the inexperienced horse by prescribing rhythm, length of stride, and distance to take-off. When not using cavalletti, all of these things are left up to the horse (with the exception of some control on the part of the rider).

A Word about In-and-Outs

One problem remains to be mentioned. Canter cavalletti are often set at intervals of one canter stride, or only 10 to 11 1/2 ft (3–3.5m), as so-called in-and-outs. Experience shows that such in-and-outs, even if they consist of nothing but low cavalletti combinations, must be dealt with very cautiously.

Many good young horses with great natural aptitude have been and continue to be injured physically and soured mentally by too much work over in-and-out combinations that are too high and consist of too many jumps (Fig. 22). There is a very logical reason for this. The springiness required by such combinations places great strain on the horse's long back. In addition, riders often lack sufficient jumping practice and lag behind or jump ahead of the motion, jarring the horse's back and creating further strain on the vertebrae and intervertebral disks. If the back muscles are not yet

Figure 22. In-and-outs like these should be avoided.

completely developed this often results in irrepa-
rable damage. The outcome, a harmful overtaxing
of the horse, is exactly the opposite of what I have
made the basic principle of my method: cavalletti
work as a gentle schooling method that guarantees
long-term productivity based on the most complete
gymnastic fitness possible. This is why, among
other things, my method generally employs a modified interval of 20ft (6m) for canter cavalletti.

6

Cavalletti Work in Traditional Riding Instruction and in Self-Instruction of Beginners

We have completed our first phase with the description of basic training over cavalletti at the walk, trot, and canter. Before we move on to more advanced cavalletti training I would like to say a few words about the use of cavalletti work in traditional riding instruction and in the self-instruction of beginners.

Traditional Riding Instruction

Normally, a novice becomes acquainted with the challenges of riding while on the back of an experienced horse. It will become obvious that this should be the case particularly if cavalletti work is to be integrated into the beginning stages of traditional instruction. It is absolutely necessary to work with a school horse that is at least trained in walk cavalletti. Beyond that it is up to the riding instructor to vary the standardized teaching format in order to foster the student's enthusiasm.

If a student has difficulty correctly positioning his or her center of gravity or staying balanced, or frequently tenses up, the instructor can try to apply a type of occupational therapy, at first using only walk cavalletti. It is the instructor's responsibility to determine to what degree the prerequisites for this, in the form of talent and willingness of the student, are present. This way the course of instruction is diversified in a way that is psychologically effective and might help rid the student of tension and bad habits. I stress might, because while this occupational therapy can achieve the desired results, it is not a cure-all. Should it have any negative effects, however, it can be stopped at any time without leaving any lasting damage.

The simplest walk cavalletti work, built into a normal program of trot work, includes the very im-

portant halt at walk, resumption of the trot, exercises in maintaining balance, and perhaps most
important of all, the natural coordination of all
movements. We will forego trot cavalletti for the
time being, as they force riders to react in coordination with a faster series of movements, and unprac-
ticed riders may have trouble maintaining equilibrium.

Self-Instruction of Beginners

Time and again, enthusiastic students who
have just learned to manage the walk, trot, and
canter ask if they may also begin cavalletti work.
The question can be answered with a yes, and we
recommend the use of cavalletti work in traditional
riding instruction. Usually, though, the question re-
lates to the fact that the opportunity for real cavalletti training is often absent. The question then becomes whether the beginner with a good grasp of
the fundamentals of riding should tackle cavalletti
training independently.

Naturally, working under the supervision of a
qualified instructor is preferable, but sometimes
one must have the courage to act independently.
The first prerequisite is that the courageous student
have access to a suitable space and a horse.
Reaching one's intended goal becomes more diffi-

cult if the horse lacks experience at cavalletti work.
In this case, the rider must approach the initial work
of familiarization (see Chap. 2) with twice as much
patience and care.

The most important preparation for self-taught
students, after reading the first chapter of this book
several times, is to go through the required movements mentally, testing themselves critically to see
if the material that has been learned theoretically
has indeed sunk in. To help determine this, students—without the book in hand, and minus the
horse—should take a close look at the cavalletti:
one low one, then two low ones set 5 to 5 1/2 ft
(1.5–1.6m) apart, followed by four more set 5 to
5 1/2 ft (1.5–1.6m) apart. If possible they should already be set up, ready and waiting, in the intended
space. This fixes the students' book learning more
firmly and vividly in the mind. Even with the proper
mental preparation, the novice who lacks a suitable
instructor will experience a certain insecurity during
initial cavalletti training. Rider and horse have to
grapple with the unfamiliar material both physically
and mentally.

The student with the right amount of self-criticism and patience will be rewarded, as one of the
results of cavalletti training is a routineness—not
automation—which otherwise takes years of practice to achieve.

It should always remain a primary rule, however, that students read and reread this book and monitor themselves critically. Self-taught riders are sure to be acquainted with someone more experienced than themselves, and I also recommend that they let that person check their progress from time to time.

7

Cavalletti Combinations at the Walk, Trot, and Canter

Mastering cavalletti work at the three basic gaits is an absolute prerequisite for the combined exercises presented on the following pages. A consistent progression—from easy to increasingly demanding and subtle—is fundamental to the structure of these gymnastic exercises and at the same time characterizes their purpose.

It is customary to start with walk cavalletti, followed by a space of six paces and four trot cavalletti. Now riders can implement everything they and

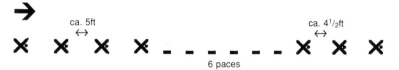

Figure 23. Combination of walk, trot, and canter cavalletti.

their horses have learned up to this point. However, the distance of only six paces between the walk and trot cavalletti puts rider and mount under time pressure. Immediately following the last walk cavalletti the rider, by straightening the upper body and pushing forward with the seat, must exercise enough control to move promptly into a sitting trot. The challenge lies in a seamless transition from the walk to the trot; at the same time, the properly timed release of the hands at the first trot cavalletti is also essential. The amount of regular schooling needed will vary with each rider's talent and aptitude, but regular practice is essential for all riders if they are to reach the level of confidence at which they can make the right move at the right time almost intuitively.

Combinations are set up in the following logical progression (all cavalletti at half height): 4 walk cavalletti/space of 6 paces/4–6 trot cavalletti/space of 6 paces/canter-distance cavalletti/space of 6 paces/canter cavalletti: 1 half-height cavalletti set on top of 1 upright cavalletti (Fig. 23). Figure 24 shows a variation with a birch pole–cavalletti oxer at the end of the sequence. As I have stated re-

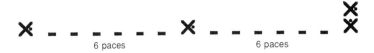

Figure 24. Combination: 4 trot cavalletti/space of 6 paces/ canter-distance cavalletti/space of 6 paces/birch pole– cavalletti oxer.

edly, walk and trot cavalletti are best dealt with in a calm, concentrated manner (Fig. 25). After the last trot cavalletti, the rider straightens the upper body and pushes forward with the seat, cantering on in such a way that the canter stride before the canter-distance cavalletti can be energetically emphasized.

The release of the hands, already practiced at the walk and trot, must now happen much more quickly in this shortened interval. The distance-cavalletti, set at half height, is ridden at the canter; the hands give elastically, the seat continues to drive the horse forward, and the torso remains up-

Figure 25. Calmness and concentration over trot cavalletti.

Figure 26. Negotiating the canter-distance cavalletti . . .

Figure 27. . . . and finding the correct take-off point.

right so that the correct take-off point for the following one-and-a-half cavalletti can be found (Fig. 26).
These two cavalletti, stacked one on top of the
other, should induce the rider to move seamlessly
into the forward jumping position (Fig. 27). Figure
28 shows an additional combination of trot and
canter cavalletti with an upright.

Again, the following should be emphasized:
After the landing the rider should straighten up as
quickly as possible and bring the cantering motion
under control by using the seat, at the same time
letting the horse move up to the bit so that continu-
ity of rider and horse is not lost.

It is important for future development that the rider make the horse accept the leg and continue in a straight line. Unfortunately, riders often turn their horses after a jump, out of carelessness or lack of ability, giving the horse repeated opportunity to escape the controlling influence of the rider and to assert its own intentions. This will make it difficult to maintain a specific line over a jumper course, and it will not be easy to correct this mistake later.

Figure 28. Combination: 4 trot cavalletti/space of 6 paces/
canter-distance cavalletti/space of 6 paces/upright: 1 upright plus 1 half-height cavalletti/space of 6 paces/upright
ca. 3 1/2 ft (1.1m) high .

8

Cavalletti Work over Curved Lines

Preparation

Horse and rider should have mastered all of the previous cavalletti exercises (walk, trot, and canter cavalletti, as well as combinations of the three) before embarking on work over cavalletti on a curved line.

To prepare for this new exercise we will use a row of four walk and then four trot cavalletti, *still set in a straight line* but placed on a large circle

(Fig. 29). This is done for two reasons. First, in this way the horse becomes accustomed to the bending later required by cavalletti set in a curve. The horse approaches the first cavalletti more or less strongly bent, goes over the row of cavalletti in an almost straight line, and then continues along the circle with an appropriate degree of bend. When this exercise is performed at the trot, the bend of the horse along the circle can be used to increase length of stride in the hindquarters; this is accomplished by employing forward-driving seat aids over the final approach strides to the first cavalletti. In this way, the cavalletti are negotiated with rhythm and natural impulsion.

The second reason for practicing first over a

Figure 29. Cavalletti set in a straight line on a large circle.

straight row of cavalletti on a circle is that it quickly becomes clear that setting up four to six cavalletti on a curved line is not exactly easy. Practice and a good eye for distance help the most, but a certain feeling for the job and an ability to visualize layout are needed in order to do justice to the potential length of stride of the individual horse.

Naturally these initial exercises should be done in both directions so that the horse is trained to bend to the right and to the left and can then, gymnastically schooled, go on to perform cavalletti work over curved lines (Fig. 30).

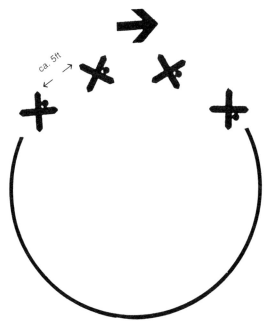

Figure 30. Cavalletti over the curved line of a circle.

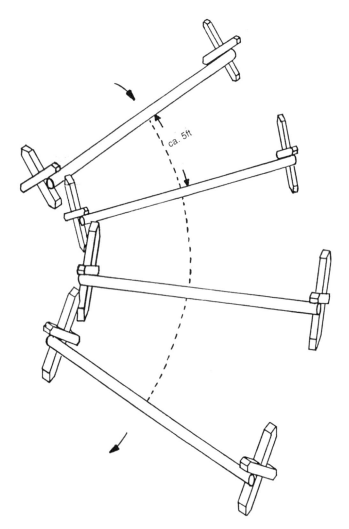

ca. 5ft

Figure 31. Curve of walk cavalletti.

Working at the Walk

Walk cavalletti over a curved line give the horse and rider a chance to get acquainted with the exercise at a true slow-motion tempo. The centrifugal force felt on the trot cavalletti curve is absent in the exercise at the walk. The direction and line of movement are not affected by it and, thus, are for the most part laid out in advance. The curve is approached and ridden over at the center of the cavalletti (Fig. 31), so the rider can concentrate completely on the sequence of movements and the horse can adjust to it calmly.

The formation shown in Figure 32 has proven a useful combination for practicing cavalletti on a curve at the walk. Four walk cavalletti are placed in

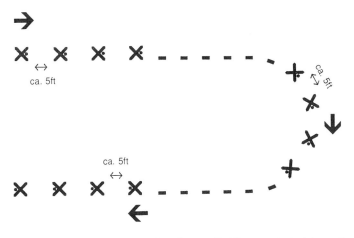

Figure 32. Combination of walk cavalletti over straight and curved lines.

a straight line, followed by a space of six paces and four to six cavalletti arranged over a 180-degree curve. These are followed by another interval of six paces and four more walk cavalletti set in a straight line.

Walk cavalletti should be practiced in both directions so that a strong foundation is laid for the following and substantially more challenging work of riding cavalletti over a curved line at the trot.

Working at the Trot

In order to successfully negotiate cavalletti over curved lines at the trot, the rider has to take into account the centrifugal force present at the trot. The goal is for the horse to go down the row of cavalletti on as uniform a curve as possible, rather than to leave the curve on a tangent, as has proven to happen easily and can be demonstrated without difficulty.

To these tactical considerations belongs familiarity with the horse's agility. The less agile a horse is, the more the curved row of, say, four cavalletti has to begin at the outside and move toward the inside, providing the less-practiced horse with a relatively straight path over the cavalletti curve. The rider can again increase the forward push of the seat immediately before the first cavalletti in order to give the horse the impulsion necessary to successfully negotiate the uneven intervals between cavalletti.

Training that progresses systematically demands more and more of the bend required for the horse to perform work correctly over curved lines. The horse should be bent around the inside driving leg, which is now applied more forcefully.

Throughout these exercises, the action of the hands—or use of the reins—should be limited to extremely discreet directional aids. Many riders are amazed to learn how important very calm familiarization work, strategy, rhythm, shifting of weight, and driving leg aids are to the success of this difficult form of gymnastic exercise.

Working over Alternating Curves

After working successfully over curved lines in both directions at the walk and trot, the next logical step is to combine curved lines to the right and the left. The interval following the first curved line of four cavalletti should be large enough that the rider can use seat contact to reestablish rhythm and balance and position the horse for the next row of cavalletti, which curves in the opposite direction (Fig. 33). Horse and rider change direction repeatedly over these alternating curves, and again confront the crucial task of correctly shifting the center

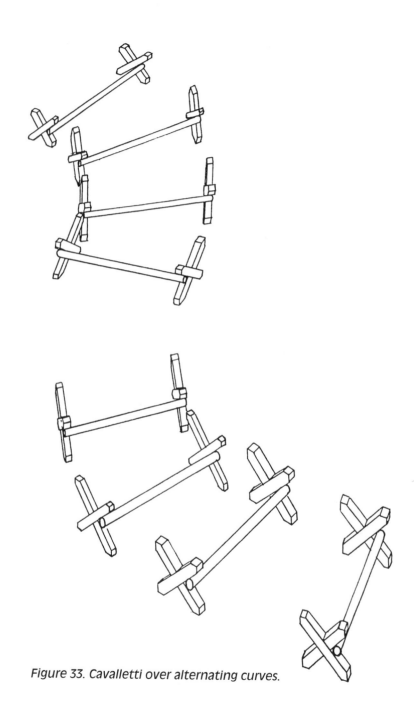

Figure 33. Cavalletti over alternating curves.

Figure 34. Alternating curves joined by a straight row of cavalletti.

of gravity while at the same time maintaining rhythm and timing.

Again, this type of schooling should make certain movements routine to horse and rider without producing a boring, automated style of riding. The trainer or rider should call on experience and imagination to vary the exercises in this part of the program to suit individual needs, for example by linking alternating trot cavalletti curves with a straight row of trot cavalletti (Fig. 34).

The transition from one cavalletti curve to another can be made more challenging with the use of a single trot jump roughly 32in (80cm) high. The distance from the landing to the next cavalletti curve should be approximately 12 paces (Fig. 35). In this interval the rider must manage to carry out such required movements as straightening the upper body and using the seat in conjunction with the properly timed transition to the trot. In a rather difficult exercise like this one this interval must give the horse enough room to make it easier for it to balance itself before the second cavalletti curve.

As the exercises become more challenging, timing becomes more crucial. The sequence of movements the rider has to carry out have become routine, but must now be prepared and executed much more quickly. The rider's intuition and the expertise of horse and rider gain importance as they build a stronger and stronger foundation for work. As we already said, this expertise should not become automation. Horse and rider face new challenges with every new situation that arises, and so

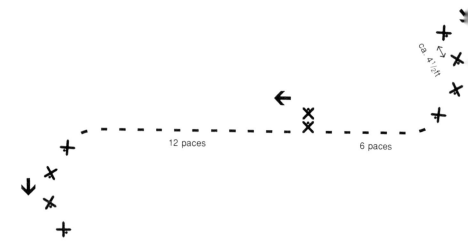

Figure 35. Alternating cavalletti curves are made more challenging by inserting an upright between them.

this diversified form of cavalletti training helps especially to elicit the fullest cooperation possible from the horse, as well as to ensure that the rider's control over his or her own actions and those of the horse remains attentive and energetic.

9

Cavalletti Work on the Longe Line

As with other types of cavalletti training, it is appropriate to begin work on the longe line at the walk. This is especially important if the horse has not yet been schooled over cavalletti on curved lines.

Four cavalletti set low or at half height are sufficient. They should be set up so that they radiate out from the circle used for longeing (compare Fig. 31). As explained in the previous chapter, setting them up requires patience and a sensitive touch. It is important that the distance of 5 to 5 1/2 ft (1.5–1.6m) between walk cavalletti be measured down the middle of the curved line. The horse is then longed to the inside or the outside of this middle line, depending on its length of stride. This makes it easier for the horse to negotiate the radial row of cavalletti. When longeing at the walk it is good to have a partner lead the horse by the halter and help it find the best line.

One more technicality of which, in my experience, riders unfortunately need to be reminded: Always run up the stirrups so they don't bounce against the horse's sides.

Side-reins must be used with caution. The horse's head should never reach a vertical position; it is preferable to have the reins too long rather than too short. When going over the cavalletti the horse should be able to stretch forward and down and to round its back. Even on the longe the horse should be urged to go into self-carriage. That is the goal of this particular kind of schooling, and the cavalletti are an aid in reaching it. Along the cavalletti-free stretch of the circle the horse reestablishes the proper timing and rhythm, and its performance over the cavalletti formation improves with each repetition.

Once the horse has fully accepted schooling on the longe at the walk, it is usually fairly easy to develop the longe work further using trot cavalletti.

Rhythm and reaction of the horse increase accordingly, demanding the full attention of the person longeing the horse. It is also important that this training, which should be carried out in both directions, last no longer than five to ten minutes.

As in longeing over cavalletti at the walk, the horse's path should ideally lead down the middle of the curved line of cavalletti. Along this middle line the intervals between cavalletti should be about 4 to 4 1/2 ft (1.3–1.4m). Again, the horse is worked to the inside or outside of the middle line, depending on its length of stride.

Having a helper lead the horse effectively is made more difficult, to say the least, by the faster tempo of the trot. The previous work at the walk, however, usually prepares the horse sufficiently to adjust skillfully to the new exercises. In general, it can be observed that a horse that is used to the cavalletti work described up to this point is also well-equipped to handle longeing over cavalletti.

Now comes the question of whether to further extend work on the longe to include canter cavalletti. I reject this practice, because I believe that the bending required by the curved lines subjects even the riderless horse to too much strain during the landing following each canter cavalletti. This could easily lead to tendon and ligament injuries. I personally disapprove of longeing with the rider in the saddle for the same reason. How far beyond walk and trot cavalletti schooling on the longe should go depends on the instructor's experience and the horse's proficiency. Again, longeing requires great calm, patience, and sensitivity of the instructor, and only a schooling program designed with foresight will give the horse confidence and fulfill the desired goals.

Cavalletti work on the longe is especially useful for convalescing horses that have suffered injuries to the back or withers (saddle sores, etc.) and cannot be ridden. We will return to this in Chapter 12.

10

The Seamless Transition to Jumping Instruction

In Chapter 5, "Cavalletti Work at the Canter," I mentioned that the exercises are a preliminary step to jumping training. Gymnastic work, over cavalletti rows and combinations at the walk, trot, and canter, gives horse and rider the confidence and security to judge distances correctly. A new challenge is presented by four trot cavalletti followed by a space of six paces and an upright cavalletti with another set at half height on top of it (Fig. 36), providing the opportunity to glide almost effortlessly into a canter

Figure 36. Simple transition from trot cavalletti to a cavalletti jump.

following the trot cavalletti, take one canter stride, and jump the obstacle with good balance.

Routinely being able to judge distance correctly has the important advantage of freeing the rider to concentrate on other matters, such as effective use of the hands and seat, and increases the self-confidence of the less-experienced horse.

Increased use of the seat before the first trot cavalletti has already been practiced many times; now it is applied very deliberately, so that this time the low fence that follows is jumped with a fluid tempo, rather than in slow motion. The tempo transition from trot cavalletti into a canter has already been practiced in basic schooling over cavalletti combinations (see Chap. 7). In this way the transition to jumping is accomplished, without (let me emphasize this again) overtaxing the horse's physical and psychological capabilities.

When the rider is ready to confront a single fence, I suggest using the combination pictured in Figure 36, followed by a wide 180-degree turn and,

Figure 37. Jumping an easier fence without the help of a distance cavalletti.

after a certain interval, an honest, low upright with wings and ground line. The familiar rhythm over the four trot cavalletti and subsequent cavalletti jump increases the horse's sense of security and self-confidence, so that after the turn (which serves to regulate the horse and bring it up to the bit) the horse is able to find the correct tempo and take-off point even without a cavalletti to help determine distance. This exercise in particular clearly shows

Figure 38. This combination demands good control over the cavalletti curve and development of forward motion over the canter combination.

what a valuable and versatile teaching tool cavalletti work is, and emphasizes as well the success of this method of schooling (Fig. 37).

Cavalletti work over combinations that include a 180-degree turn has already been practiced (compare Fig. 32); this work will now be incorporated into the current phase of schooling. Figure 38 shows how the cavalletti should be set up. A curved line of four trot cavalletti leads into the 180-degree turn; the turn, measured over a distance of about nine paces, is followed by a distance cavalletti set at half height. This in turn is followed by a space of six paces and a jump consisting of an upright cavalletti with another set at half height on top of it. The curved line of trot cavalletti limits tempo and impulsion at the trot, forcing horse and rider to negotiate the canter combination with rela-

Figure 39. Oxer with top front cavalletti at half height to make it more inviting, followed by a space of 12 paces in which tempo is regulated, and a row of trot cavalletti.

tively little impulsion as well. The goal of this exercise lies in maintaining good control over the curve of trot cavalletti, as well as developing sufficient forward motion over the canter combination.

It is up to the trainer to tailor the jump or cavalletti formations to meet individual needs. For instance, a cavalletti in-and-out with an interval of only three paces can be substituted for the canter combination with a six-pace interval. Once again, however, let me emphasize that in-and-outs should be used as seldom as possible, and never when dealing with inexperienced horses and riders. The most important aspects of this were discussed in the section of Chapter 5 titled "A Word about In-and-Outs." Because of its modest dimensions, the combination given above as an example is not likely to cause any harm or injury when used within the framework of cavalletti schooling; but it is always the trainer's responsibility to keep the quantity and quality of such combinations under control.

A very effective exercise for increasing the

Figure 40. First jump of the exercise pictured in Figure 39.

horse's responsiveness is one that uses a small square oxer roughly 3 1/2 ft (1m) high and 3 1/2 ft (1m) wide, followed by an interval of twelve paces and four trot cavalletti (Fig. 40). For novice horses and riders, I recommend making the oxer more inviting by setting the top front cavalletti at half height (Fig. 39) or replacing the entire oxer with a jump of one upright and one half-height cavalletti. As training progresses the interval can be reduced from twelve to eight paces.

At first the oxer or cavalletti formation should be approached at a trot. Once this is done successfully and the horse demonstrates responsiveness when being brought back to the trot before the row of cavalletti, horse and rider can progress to practicing the approach to the oxer at a canter. Among other things, these exercises are designed to test and improve the rider's reactions and the horse's readiness to respond.

Further challenges can be presented by making the canter cavalletti more difficult, but even then I recommend starting out with a row of four trot cavalletti. This can then be followed by a space of six paces and a transition to the canter over a jump of one-and-a-half cavalletti; another six-pace interval and a low canter-distance cavalletti; a space of six or seven paces and a square oxer (two cavalletti high and two cavalletti deep); an interval of six paces and a one-and-a-half cavalletti; a 180-degree turn over approximately twelve paces; another canter-distance cavalletti, followed by a space of six or seven paces and a final jump of two upright and one half-height cavalletti stacked on top of each other (Fig. 41).

It should go without saying that despite their modest proportions such combinations should not be jumped more than twice at a time. It is useful later to alter the formation so that the cavalletti are ridden over in the opposite direction. Naturally, this necessitates moving the cavalletti and setting them up all over again. Figure 42 shows that the four trot cavalletti then form the start on the right, and the highest cavalletti jump again comes at the end of the sequence. Don't forget to pace out the correct

Figure 41. Schooling becomes more demanding when several cavalletti jumps are added to the combination.

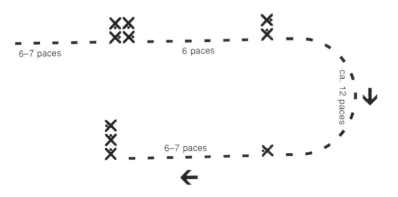

Figure 42. Same combination as pictured in Figure 41, but in the opposite direction.

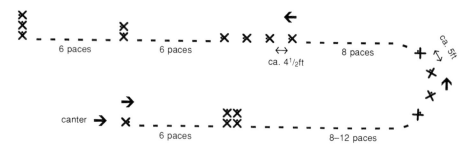

Figure 43. This combination demands a lot of responsiveness and elasticity of the horse.

distances between obstacles again, and to make sure that all upper cavalletti that are set at half-height face in the new direction.

Here is another exercise, one that demands a great deal of responsiveness and elasticity on the part of the horse: canter-distance cavalletti, ridden at canter on the left lead; space of six paces and a square oxer about 3 1/2 ft (1m) by 3 1/2 ft (1m); interval of eight or twelve paces and a 180-degree turn to the left over four walk cavalletti; space of eight paces and four trot cavalletti; space of six paces and a jump of one upright and one half-height cavalletti; space of six paces and a final jump of two and a half cavalletti (Fig. 43).

Style Refinement

At this level of training it is natural that gradually more and more emphasis is placed on a stylistically pure execution of the last practice phase, especially the jump.

I do not advocate working over upright cavalletti at a walk or trot (other than when schooling already advanced dressage horses, which, however, has little in common with the schooling of other young riding and sport horses). We should never forget that it is not easy for the horse to maintain the proper timing over the intervals between cavalletti while carrying the rider.

The experience of carrying out the series of movements at a faster pace provides the first opportunity for riders to evaluate their own coordination as well as that of their horses, to make corrections where necessary, and possibly to use it to refine their style. In the latter case, now is the time to influence more deliberately the last phase before the row of cavalletti. Up to now, importance was placed on an emphatic straightening of the torso for a better forward-driving seat in the last trot strides before the cavalletti. Now the experienced trainer can try permitting the student a lighter, slightly forward-leaning posture (Fig. 44), which facilitates a very fluid transition to the suspended seat. The forward drive of the seat, however, must be maintained, as successful negotiation of the cavalletti depends on this. This should make clear to the practiced and talented student the ideal take-off position that will later be used over fences on a jumper course.

Figure 44. Maintaining forward drive of the seat while leaning slightly forward over the cavalletti.

11

Cavalletti Work as Gymnastic Exercise for the Experienced Jumper before, during, and after Competition

The tremendous physical and psychological demands of modern jumping competition mean that a horse needs not only the best possible predisposition for the sport but also complete gymnastic fitness. It is almost impossible to introduce a horse to more demanding exercises through uninterrupted jumping work and at the same time to keep it sound. Even if muscles and tendons survive this strain without damage, the psychological stress is almost guaranteed to nip progress and carefully maintained fitness in the bud. A famous rider once said, "Every jumper has a certain number of jumps in it—that number could be five hundred or it could be forty thousand. If you take them out too early all you are left with is the skin, so to speak." That may sound somewhat exaggerated, but it is absolutely true. One thing is certain: Thousands of young jumpers with great potential have been ruined, because they tried to do too much for their age.

Only the most complete but considerate gymnastic exercise—and not jumping, jumping, and more jumping—can help meet the challenges of today's competitions. Instead of subjecting the horse to additional stress with schooling that is just as demanding as competition, riders should take advantage of the special benefits of cavalletti training to give their horses the gymnastic exercise they need. It provides a basis for continued success by calming the horse psychologically and gently promoting recuperation of the organs, muscles, tendons, and ligaments taxed in the last competition. The distances this book prescribes for walk, trot, and canter cavalletti do not drain the horse's strength. They instill trust, and, thus, allow restorative training that makes full use of every aspect of the horse's constitution yet rules out the stress, including the psychological strain, of jumping training that mirrors competition.

As long as there are no acute leg injuries, it is appropriate to practice a simple form of light walk and trot cavalletti work for about ten minutes on the day following a competition. This should be done only on the condition that the horse is already familiar with cavalletti work and has performed it willingly in the past. This rhythmic, light movement provides the needed relaxation. In addition, the entire body and most importantly the muscles, tendons, and ligaments most taxed in competition benefit from a general increase in circulation and are freed of any remaining buildup of lactic acid.

It is definitely not necessary to incorporate jump combinations into the cavalletti sequence for the first two days. Again, it is up to the trainer or experienced rider to decide when to increase the work load in this way. Very often the principle that "less is sometimes more" should be kept firmly in mind. Important in every case is that the cavalletti distances between and in front of obstacles be tailored to fit the capacity of the individual horse. Whether and how to start jumping small fences at a trot is a further decision the rider or trainer must make.

A word of advice, especially for younger riders, is never to school over jumps larger than two-thirds the height of those used in competition. Very often riders want to compensate for their hang-ups or fears of a competition course by jumping higher and wider obstacles in training or even in the warm-up ring. Unfortunately, the prevailing opinion is often "If I jump fences 5ft (1.5m) high and wide in schooling, it will be that much easier to master a novice's course."

When designing a program of restorative training the decisive question is naturally often how much time remains until the next planned competition. If only a few days remain, as is often the case during show season, emphasis should, as previously mentioned, be placed on mental recuperation, and physical demands should be limited to light cavalletti work. A longer break between competitions allows variable and increasingly demanding cavalletti work. Depending on the individual situation this can be made more challenging with appropriate cavalletti combinations, for example a trot-canter cavalletti combination followed by small triples and a 180-degree turn with four trot cavalletti.

Instead of the triples the practicing rider can, of course, use any kind of obstacle or combination that is likely to create difficulty in competition, but should never forget that these should be only two-thirds as high and wide as the competition obstacles are expected to be.

Finally, a word about cavalletti work for horses that are coming out of a heavy competition schedule and will be given a long rest. The first week following heavy competition should be devoted to cross-country training, but without any notable stress. Calm work at all three basic gaits, some of it on a longer rein, is best for healing the horse's psyche, tendons, and muscles, and for restoring normal suppleness and looseness.

In the second week, a simple form of trot cavalletti schooling can be started. About ten minutes out of every hour of work should be devoted to this. Toward the end of the week, work over canter cavalletti (but not in-and-outs) can be taken up. Rows of cavalletti at all three gaits can be linked as long as intervals of proper size are emphasized so that suppleness and looseness, forward impulsion, and rhythm can be maintained. Pay attention to the horse's reactions; the horse should be content and calm and, as always should be rewarded with lots of vocal praise and pats.

12

Training Resumption and Gymnastic Exercising of the Convalescing Horse

Every rider will confirm that resuming schooling of an injured horse after a short or longer period of rest is a tricky matter. The horse's natural temperament plays a decisive role, especially in the first phase of training resumption.

The period of rest and lack of circulation naturally make injured tendons, muscles, and ligaments more sensitive to sudden strain, but even uninjured parts of the body are susceptible to harm. If necessary, side-reins can be used at first to help intercept and regulate any overly strong reactions on the part of the horse. If a certain degree of suppleness and looseness returns after a few days of careful movement therapy, then cavalletti work at a walk can be included in the recuperative program. No matter what the circumstances, though, the rider's intentions must be discussed with a veterinarian and work should not resume until the veterinarian has approved it.

As previously mentioned, schooling over walk cavalletti can be an especially worthwhile part of the program. Unless the horse has back injuries that prevent it from being worked under saddle and that limit schooling to work on the longe (see Chap. 9), several goals can be achieved simultaneously through the calm, rhythmic, and gentle action of the walk cavalletti. The entire tendon, ligament, and muscle structure of the extremities, as well as the neck and shoulder region, are revived by increased circulation. Balance and equilibrium between horse and rider are restored, which has a positive psychological effect. All of this contributes to a faster recovery. Exactly how much time is spent on walk cavalletti as part of a program of recuperative work is left to the judgment and sensitivity of the rider, but it should be no more than ten minutes.

It is understandable that walk cavalletti work may seem boring because of the cavalletti formations and the less than dramatic nature of the work.

Figure 45. For convalescing horses: a simple combination of walk and trot cavalletti.

The rider should remember, however, that a great deal of time and money was spent on the horse's recovery. This small additional test of patience is therefore hardly worth mentioning, especially as it will make the recovery time three to four times shorter. And, if the animal in question is a competition horse, the benefits of the gymnastic exercise the horse simultaneously receives will show when competition is begun again.

If the horse's condition improves markedly, work over trot cavalletti can begin after a few days. This work is especially successful when used in conjunction with walk cavalletti (Fig. 45).

Always make sure that any schooling is appropriate to the horse's level of convalescence; work with restraint. Cavalletti training over curved lines should not be used at first, as the strain would be too great. Canter cavalletti should also be used only sparingly and for specific purposes, and only after the veterinarian has evaluated the horse's condition and is convinced that the horse is fit enough for the springiness that these exercises require. Again, I recommend combining these with walk and trot cavalletti (Fig. 46). Even after the horse is again able to withstand a good deal of strain, one should refrain from performing 180-degree turns at a   canter.

Finally, let me once again impress upon the reader that for the convalescent horse, only carefully considered and moderate use of cavalletti work leads to a successful restoration of health and resumption of training.

Figure 46. For horses in an advanced stage of convalescence: a combination of walk, trot, and canter cavalletti.

13

Using Cavalletti to Lengthen Stride

It goes without saying that when purchasing a horse the primary considerations are breeding, conformation and constitution, and any easily recognizable traits. This is especially true when buying horses intended for a special purpose, like dressage horses and jumpers, whose conformation and movement show promise for the particular requirements of that kind of competition. Important prerequisites for dressage horses are the stride and natural balance; combined training horses and jumpers should also exhibit certain physical and psychological qualities. Certainly, though, the demand for *length of stride* is shared by all.

The horse should show a certain length of stride under saddle even when collected. However, in many cases this quality needs improving. We can expect well-directed cavalletti work to lead to marked progress in this area, especially with horses whose conformation and resulting length of stride restrict the normal walk and trot. In such cases the ability of the horse being schooled should be considered when setting up walk cavalletti. Instead of using the 5 to 5 1/2 ft (1.5–1.6m) intervals previously prescribed, set the cavalletti only so far apart that the practice row can just be negotiated with a steady rhythm, maintaining as before an interval large enough so that the horse can set each foot down once in each interval. This spacing is a very individual matter.

After these close-set cavalletti have been successfully negotiated a number of times the intervals can be increased a bit, by about 2 to 4in (5–10cm). There is no absolute norm for this increase. In order to overcome the increased distance with the same rhythm but a necessarily longer stride, the rider must increase forward drive through the seat to animate the horse so that it correctly negotiates the approach to the first cavalletti. Should the horse lose impulsion, it is up to the rider to restore this through a driving lower leg and simultaneous use of the voice, so that the cavalletti can be ridden in the desired manner. Talented and experienced riders can easily determine the degree to which the aids should be used, but inexperienced riders need the support of an instructor who can tell them when to apply the necessary aids.

In this way, length of stride is gradually increased. Still, this training does have limits that are determined by the individual horse, and again it is up to the instructor to take into account the ability and willingness of the horse and to vary the program accordingly.

To lengthen the stride further, increase the number of cavalletti from the usual four to eight and even twelve, if available. The first four trot cavalletti should be set at normal intervals, the following somewhat further apart. The impulsion gained over the first four cavalletti helps the horse negotiate the successive intervals with more extension.

In the next stage, the following sequence is used: four trot cavalletti, set somewhat further apart from each other (the distance having been increased to suit the individual horse); a space of six paces followed by an oxer roughly 32in (80cm) high and 3 1/2 ft (1m) wide; and a space of twelve paces followed once again by four trot cavalletti set as far apart as possible. This combination of trot cavalletti/jump/trot cavalletti with individually determined wider spacing prompts the horse to stretch and increase its length of stride in all the phases.

The influence of the seat in the approach to the trot cavalletti is obvious by now, but I mention it again because it is what drives the horse to negotiate the increased intervals rhythmically and flawlessly. In this exercise special attention should be paid to perfect coordination of the hands when jumping the square oxer at a trot.

This cavalletti training, aimed at improving length of stride, will not work miracles, but with steady use improvement should be noticeable after about four weeks.

14

Reschooling the High-Strung Horse

I would like to say here in advance that it is a typical human trait to look for the root of a problem everywhere but with one's self. This becomes a problem when a living creature—in this case the horse—is the target of our dissatisfaction. One has to assume that most means used to try to reschool overly spirited or violent horses, or, to put it plainly, to force them into obedience, are of little use.

A horse that is talented but nevertheless uncooperative when it comes to work, for whatever reason, must be trained carefully using a combination of friendliness and firmness. This well-known fact is often ignored. We should use applied psychology to create the basis for a quieting therapy for each individual horse. This is the perfect opportunity for trainers and riding instructors to prove their expertise and love of their chosen field. Success depends on patience and sensitivity paired with professional knowledge. It can never be achieved through brute strength, toughness, and thoughtless use of force; these will never inspire a sensitive horse with the confidence it needs to cooperate the way we want it to.

I recommend that riders and trainers draw up a plan tailored to the horse in question, naturally with an emphasis on quieting it. The only rules that apply to every case are very general; success lies in the details of the individually adapted schooling. This places special demands on the ability and character of the riding instructor or trainer, who has to alter or redesign the program if it does not prove successful. This requires courage and self-criticism in addition to professional ability.

It is assumed that the professionally educated trainer will carry out the initial quieting program. The trainer should employ psychological tactics and physical aids: influence of the hand, leg, and seat, coordinated with vocal praise. Schooling is done over walk, trot, and canter cavalletti and continues until the horse's action can be regulated as completely as possible over a jumper course.

As I said before, it is very difficult—perhaps impossible—to put a fixed training program down on paper. I will give some examples that should be modified for the individual horse, but that contain the basic elements of every training process.

The trainer's most important consideration should be the age and level of instruction of the horse in question. Trainers can usually accustom younger horses to the rider's aids in a short period of time by using good conventional schooling methods and treating the horses with constant friendliness. This is not true of older animals that have often had more or less negative experiences and as a result are filled with fear, insecurity, and mistrust.

Here the primary goal is to win back the horse's trust no matter what. Maintaining an especially amiable attitude, rewarding the horse repeatedly with pats and a soothing voice, and cavalletti work—for the time being at walk and trot—are appropriate means for reestablishing a basis of trust. After careful familiarization with the seat, aids, and voice of the rider at the walk and trot (but not at an extended sitting trot, which would only provoke more aggressive behavior), a quieting routine over one to four low cavalletti can soon begin. If after initial success these settling and trust-building gymnastic exercises are continued over a row of four half-height walk cavalletti and then over a simple combination of walk and trot cavalletti, then a foundation has been laid for the horse's training.

At this point we should remind ourselves of everything we have read about work over walk and trot cavalletti as pertains to the point of position, upper body position and seat aids, the phase of suspension, coordinated movement of the hands, and so on. The trot, which is usually lively and perhaps also rushed, should be normalized and brought to the proper tempo by sitting during the trot strides that follow. Only then can the rider move on at a rising trot. At the same time the rider should pat the horse reassuringly, starting at the approach and continuing until over the last walk or trot cavalletti. Naturally, this requires a free hand, and executing it depends on the rider's skill. It is important that the rider take both reins in the other hand in such a way that the horse can use its neck freely over the cavalletti. Additional soothing use of the voice is very effective. Although these actions may seem trivial and boring, they represent almost the only proper approach for reestablishing trust. Schooling over canter cavalletti should be excluded for the time being, because the forward drive it causes is likely to get out of hand.

As previously mentioned, coordination plays an important role if one action is to complement or lead smoothly into the next. In my experience, this kind of quieting program is almost always successful and can also serve as a strong foundation for subsequent jumping training.

One of the pleas for help one hears most frequently from less-experienced riders culminates in the lament, "My horse goes charging off before every jump, and after the jump is impossible to rein in!" If this is the case an additional exercise is useful: A trot jump about 24 to 32in (60–80cm) high is placed right before a turn or corner that is followed by a series of four trot cavalletti. The distance from the trot jump through the turn and to the first cavalletti should be approximately eight to twelve paces (Fig. 47).

I emphasize again that the prerequisite for this work is basic instruction that has made possible a sound execution of transitions from the canter to the trot and the trot to the walk. What helps the most in this exercise, however, is not only the rider's voice and praising pats but the turn that follows shortly after the landing. It is the rider's job to straighten the upper body immediately after the landing, thereby activating the influence of the seat. Quarter halts are then introduced, and together with increased closure of the legs and greater influence of the seat they induce the horse to glide into a trot. Remaining seated at the trot brings about not only an adjustment of the overly forward-rushing trot, but

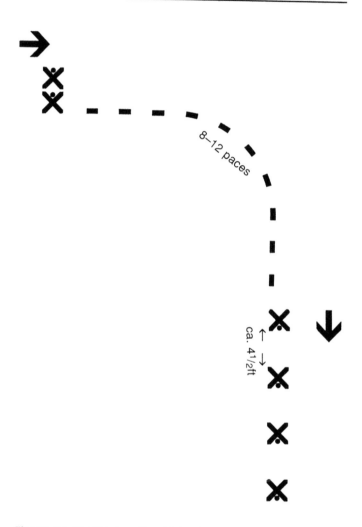

Figure 47. For reschooling high-strung horses: trot jump 24 to 32in (60–80cm) high/90-degree turn in 12, later 8 paces/ 4 half-height trot cavalletti.

also the composure required to negotiate the subsequent trot cavalletti.

Once several such turns have been performed successfully in both directions, the exercise can be repeated on a straight line (Fig. 48 and 49). The distance from the trot jump to the four trot cavalletti should measure twelve paces at first, but can later be reduced to eight. In the beginning, it is best to use low cavalletti when schooling horses with little cavalletti experience. As they become more familiar with the cavalletti these can be raised to half height.

Only when the rider or trainer can again see lasting improvement—when the horse's urge to rush forward can be largely controlled—may trot work over single fences up to approximately 3 1/2 ft (1m) high begin. In this exercise, the rider brings the horse back to the trot following every successful trot jump and then executes a volte at a purely timed trot before heading the horse toward the next fence. In this way courses with single jumps (but no combinations) can be negotiated without giving the horse a chance to "take the rider by the hand" and charge off again.

If up until now the horse has accepted the training calmly, the logical next step is jumping training at the canter. Extreme caution should be exercised here so that the progress made in calming the horse is not disrupted or perhaps even destroyed by the rider's impatience.

We can start once again with a similar se-

Figure 48. Reschooling high-strung horses: Taking the jump actively . . .

Figure 49. . . . and the trot cavalletti calmly.

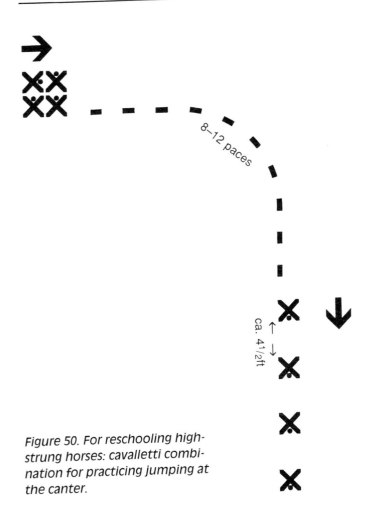

Figure 50. For reschooling high-strung horses: cavalletti combination for practicing jumping at the canter.

quence: canter over cavalletti oxer with the top front cavalletti set at half height to make the jump more inviting; 90-degree turn in twelve, later eight paces; and four half-height trot cavalletti (Fig. 50).

Of course, the transitions back to the trot must be executed more quickly and intensely, and even more attention should be paid to keeping them low and not permitting them to be carried out with raised hands and long reins "in the rider's stomach," as is often when riders are pressed for time.

Following the same pattern of exercises as that previously described for trot cavalletti, the rider, seated and with an erect torso, should execute a volte at canter after each jump and before approaching the next obstacle. Obviously, the distances between fences should be kept large enough so that even after a volte the next jump can be approached calmly. If the horse in question is schooled over the rows of various cavalletti combinations in the manner described, I am certain that it can be controlled over a jump course.

In general, I would like to add that there has been much talk and discussion about the approach to jumps. As far as riding an approach on a horse that needs correcting is concerned, the statement "Don't jump the gun!" is more valid than ever. Specifically, this means that the rider should not irritate the horse too early with the driving aids, but should instead wait until two or at most three canter strides before the obstacle before "riding forward," and naturally should do so only after first exerting control with the seat as appropriate at the canter. This should be considered when dealing with a horse that pulls or rushes. One can't work solely with technical facts but must use a little psychology as well. In this situation that means doing everything possible to completely suppress any further flare-ups of wild behavior. That is why an especially quiet influence of the seat and simultaneous elastic release of the hands in the direction of the horse's mouth after each landing are so important over a jump course. Support, or forward riding, does not commence until at the point of position for the next jump. If possible, I recommend riding the intervals between jumps with a steady but upright torso, in order to keep the action as calm as possible over the entire course.

This calming therapy can be stretched over a period of about four weeks. Two days out of every week should be devoted to hacking cross-country to prevent monotony and keep horse and rider from developing a blinkered attitude toward their work. These rides should be dominated by long gallops at a speed of 330yd (300m)/minute, ridden with a light seat. It is also important to make these outings alone, in order to avoid tempting the horse to chase after others.

Finally, I would like to emphasize that success is ensured only by regular and individually tailored work over the rows of practice cavalletti described here.

Figures 51, 52, and 53 show additional combinations with cavalletti jumps.

Figure 51. For reschooling high-strung horses: 4 half-height trot cavalletti/space of ca. 15 paces with 180-degree turn, for regulating tempo/oxer/upright/oxer, all at standard jumper course interval of 7 paces.

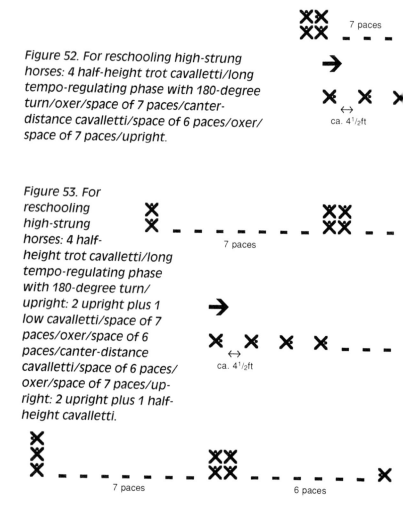

Figure 52. For reschooling high-strung horses: 4 half-height trot cavalletti/long tempo-regulating phase with 180-degree turn/oxer/space of 7 paces/canter-distance cavalletti/space of 6 paces/oxer/ space of 7 paces/upright.

Figure 53. For reschooling high-strung horses: 4 half-height trot cavalletti/long tempo-regulating phase with 180-degree turn/ upright: 2 upright plus 1 low cavalletti/space of 7 paces/oxer/space of 6 paces/canter-distance cavalletti/space of 6 paces/ oxer/space of 7 paces/up-right: 2 upright plus 1 half-height cavalletti.

7 paces

ca. 4$^{1}/_{2}$ft

7 paces

ca. 4$^{1}/_{2}$ft

7 paces

6 paces

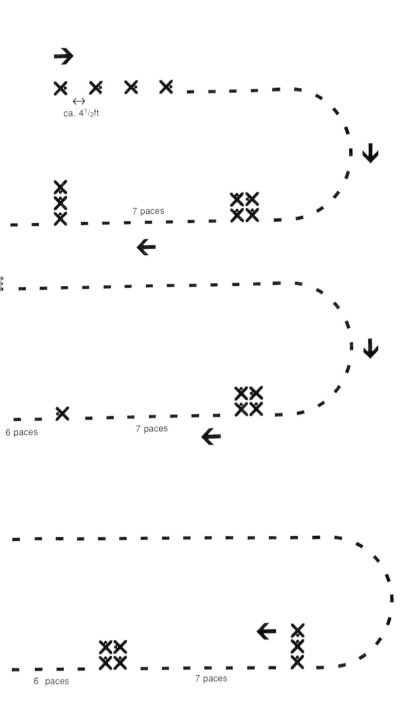

ca. 4¹/₂ft

7 paces

6 paces   7 paces

6 paces   7 paces

15

Reschooling
the Lazy Horse

In my opinion, this is a problem in which the rider's temperament plays a role: whether a rider prefers very nimble horses that often may be a bit too spirited, or horses that need some urging forward. Not every rider is well-suited for controlling excitable horses, to successfully tackle problems of a forward-driving nature. On the other hand, many riders find it difficult to restore impulsion lost, for example, over combinations. Personally, I find the lazy horse more difficult, all the more so because style and timing suffer when strong forward-driving aids must be used, and this leads to agitation.

Cavalletti work provides us with a possibility to develop these "tired" horses with forward impulsion by taking advantage, so to speak, of their instinct for self-preservation.

A horse that is already accustomed to cavalletti work can be schooled over trot and canter cavalletti combinations; these should make it easier for the horse to develop the impulsion needed to negotiate subsequent obstacles or combinations. For this purpose, four cavalletti are set up at the prescribed intervals of about 4 1/2 ft (1.35m), but the following canter cavalletti are set further apart than normal. In addition, the last canter cavalletti jump, an oxer with the top front cavalletti set at half height, should animate the horse so that it moves with impulsion and an especially long stride. The distance of seven paces between trot and canter cavalletti is more than sufficient to make a fluid transition to the canter with the help of back, leg, and voice aids, and to jump the oxer energetically.

When it seems the driving aids have made the horse aware of the forward impulsion that is required, it is time to move on to the next exercise. It begins the same way, but the cavalletti jump is different. An upright without a ground line or other aids to make it inviting, and no higher than roughly 3 1/2 ft (1m), is substituted for the easier oxer, and is followed by a space of six paces and another cavalletti oxer (Fig. 54). Now the emphasis is on taking the cavalletti jump energetically so that enough impulsion is found for the subsequent oxer. Once this exercise is performed satisfactorily, the distance between the upright and the oxer can be expanded to seven paces.

Thus, even the lazy horse learns to react to the driving aids between jumps, and to find the confidence needed to locate the right take-off point. This schooling fulfills the requirement that the horse react more promptly to the rider's aids over the course, and through this that it achieve and maintain forward impulsion.

Of course, reading a description of corrective therapy like this is easier than putting it into practice. Making the right decision in borderline cases depends on the rider's judgment, although here again somewhat "less" will sometimes be preferable as far as the degree of difficulty of the formations used is concerned.

Simple canter-distance cavalletti should be used again and again between the trot and canter cavalletti combinations. The rider canters over this

Figure 54. For reschooling lazy horses: Combination of trot and canter cavalletti, all intervals 6 paces.

distance cavalletti with an upright torso and an especially strong seat while at the same time releasing the reins. The success of this therapy is con-
firmed when horse and rider can successfully negotiate the combination pictured in Figure 55.

The most important factor is that every canter
stride, including the one over the half-height distance cavalletti, is supported in a forward-driving
manner with supple influence of the seat. In this
way the horse adapts its canter stride to the increased distance, and the forward drive is increased. This impulsion-producing exercise, together with the trot/canter combinations described
earlier, can be practiced for intervals of up to half
an hour, but should be done only about twice a
week. Normally the positive effects of this reschooling should become evident after about one
month.

*Figure 55. For reschooling lazy horses: Combination of
trot and canter cavalletti with standard jumper course
intervals of 7–8 paces.*

16

Reschooling
the Sour Horse

One of the most difficult tasks is rehabilitating the horse that has been frightened by people and made sour, and reintroducing it to general work or competition. The all-important trust between horse and rider has broken down, and it is very hard to repair this extensive damage with the usual means. A type of occupational therapy can help a little by diverting attention from the current problems. In this situation, gentle work over cavalletti provides a means for restoring the horse's self-assurance and slowly compensating for the horse's lost confidence in the rider; it puts horse and rider back on track. The calm, rhythmical work over trot and canter cavalletti combinations provides the horse with "programmed" success, and with that comes trust in the rider's actions. The voice is also an especially helpful tool, as no attempt at establishing familiarity with a horse can succeed without it. A horse that is occupied in this way can gradually be exposed to more demanding work, which in turn promotes its rehabilitation.

There is no standard pattern for this therapy, but it certainly cannot hurt to begin each lesson by letting horse and rider reach an understanding by schooling over four half-height trot cavalletti; the work should be accompanied by soothing use of the voice. A small jump six paces from the trot cavalletti marks the beginning of the rehabilitation. It is crucial, however, to avoid anything risky until the horse's trust has been strengthened enough by the cavalletti work that it will not crumble under strain.

As long as the intervals in the cavalletti rows determine the trot or canter stride, the danger of refusal remains small. The regularity of the motion becomes routine for the horse, and this affects the jumping phase in particular. The key to success lies in this regularity. Increasing these challenges slowly builds a foundation for continued reschooling. As I already emphasized, the praising and calming voice of the rider provides the horse with tremendously important psychological support; once the horse is used to it, it can compensate for any increase in stress.

If the success achieved over rows of cavalletti followed by small fences proves to be lasting, the rider can try the following. Singles or combinations that the horse has refused in the past should be duplicated as closely as possible with modest proportions—a height and spread of about 3 1/2 ft (1m)—and set up about 35ft (10m) after a canter combination. The canter combination makes the horse more confident about judging distances, and this later facilitates the successful negotiation of single fences and combinations.

When repeated success at this stage gives riders the go-ahead, they can move on to jumping various single fences and combinations that are not preceded by cavalletti, as long as they restrict themselves to very low jumps. Riders should always use especially honest fences when schooling horses that have been soured mentally. The distances for combinations should be absolutely correct and the jumps should be a maximum of two-thirds the height and width of those expected in upcoming competition.

Again, the principle to keep in mind with all of these exercises is to avoid doing anything risky during the period of rehabilitation. Each phase should start out at a maximum of half the intensity of the next. The success of this program depends on giving the horse time to adjust to the increased demands of the schooling. If setbacks occur, do not react emotionally and punish the horse; only patience, friendliness, and careful repetition of less demanding work will lead to success. This reschooling period demands that the rider be extremely patient, as well as willing and able to think ahead while adjusting to each new situation.

If the individual case demands it, a capable and sensitive rider or trainer can apply the examples shown in Figures 56 and 57. They do not, however, offer an absolute guarantee of success.

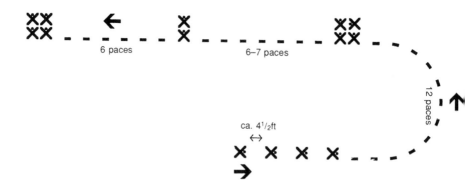

Figure 56. For reschooling sour horses: 4 half-height trot cavalletti/180-degree turn in 12 paces/oxer with top front cavalletti set at half height/space of 6–7 paces/upright: 2 upright cavalletti.

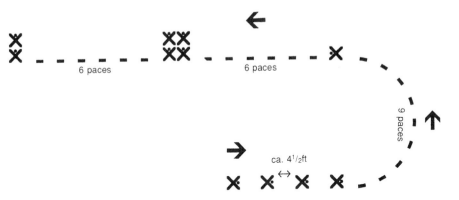

6 paces   6 paces

9 paces

ca. 4¹/₂ft

Figure 57. For reschooling sour horses: Same beginning as in Figure 56; canter-distance cavalletti following the turn/ spaces of 6 paces/oxer ca. 3 1/2 ft (1m) x 3 1/2 ft (1m)/space of 6 paces/upright: 2 upright cavalletti.

17

Training
the Green Horse

Naturally, I recommend cavalletti work wholeheartedly for training green horses. Because of this
I should perhaps add that the foundation for this is
conventional basic instruction. Of course, the
young horse should first learn the three basic gaits
and get accustomed to the rider's weight. I suggest
that well-directed cavalletti work then be used to
help the horse with the very essential task of finding and maintaining its balance.

Although it may seem logical to start with
simple walk cavalletti, the lack of impulsion inherent
in this work sometimes makes it difficult for the

horse to cope with the rider's weight and the cavalletti at the same time. The young horse should be
introduced to low cavalletti in the manner outlined
in Chapter 3. In this case, however, it is important
to go into a trot following one or two low walk
cavalletti, and to continue working at a rising trot for
several minutes before coming back to a walk and
repeating the exercise. Obviously, during this work
it is very helpful to talk to the horse and pat it reassuringly.

Breaking in a young horse is one of the most
difficult phases of training. Patience and caution
must be emphasized here, and naturally that ap-
plies to cavalletti work as well. Once in a while an
untrained horse has so much to offer that the rider
loses the proper perspective; in cavalletti work,
even very gifted horses must be brought along
slowly and carefully in order to avoid overtaxing
them. I can illustrate this with an extreme example:
I once had the "pleasure" of reschooling young
horses that had been broken in with the help of
draw-reins. It took months to get them to forget
everything they had learned from this inept application of force, but the intervals between the cavalletti
helped them gain proper rhythm and balance, and
created a fundamental unity between horse and
rider.

It is not necessary to spend more than about
five minutes out of each day's schooling on walk

cavalletti. Later, when schooling is expanded to include trot cavalletti, this can be extended to ten
minutes, but it should be done no more that two or
three times a week. Here, too, once the horse is
thoroughly familiar with the exercise the level of difficulty can be increased. Walk cavalletti followed by
a space of six paces and four low trot cavalletti are
quite sufficient for accomplishing this. The intervals
should exactly fit the walk and trot strides of the
horse in question. Once mastered, the cavalletti
can be raised to half height. It is extremely important to protect the young horse's legs with boots.

The schooling over canter cavalletti is almost
identical to that described in detail in Chapter 5. A
low canter-distance cavalletti should be used, followed by a space of six paces and an upright
cavalletti with another at half height placed directly
in front of it to make the jump more inviting (Fig.

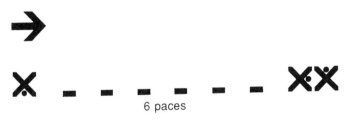

6 paces

Figure 58. Simple canter combination, especially helpful for instilling trust in the inexperienced horse.

58). The horse is brought to a canter just enough in advance that the rider can bring the action under control through discreet use of the back and the driving aids, and, most importantly, can control the negotiation of the canter-distance cavalletti.

18

Design and Construction of Cavalletti

Cavalletti should be as light as is practicable, inviting in appearance, safe to use, and built to last. In the course of many years of practical experience I have had a chance to use and compare cavalletti of widely varied constructions, some acceptable, some totally unacceptable.

Cavalletti with extremely long side pieces must be viewed especially critically. Let me repeat the warning that these can cause life-threatening injuries to horse and rider should either of them fall.

Cavalletti that are too tall are dangerous even when set at half height, and cause insecurity and muscle tension in less-experienced horses. There were also cavalletti on the market that were so enormously heavy that it was difficult for young riders or horsewomen to adjust them, let alone to carry them.

With these deficiencies in mind and with the help of Mr. Volker Lerch, an ambitious rider from Vienna, I succeeded in constructing a cavalletti that combines all of the desired qualities. It is lightweight, durable, and most importantly safe for horse and rider, as well as simple and inexpensive to construct.

Each cavalletti cross consists of two long side pieces that come to a right-angled point at either end, as well as four short pieces that are likewise pointed on one end but are straight on the other (Fig. 59a). One long piece and two short pieces are aligned at the pointed ends and then glued as well as nailed together using three nails (Fig. 59b and 60). The two long pieces are then joined at the gap between the short pieces to form a cross (Fig. 59c and 61). A round wooden pole about 10ft (3m) long and 3 1/2 to 4in (8–10cm) in diameter is placed between the two crosses. Two holes are bored into each end of the pole. The pole is then fastened to the cross at each end using two six-inch spikes. Each spike is driven through the pole and into one

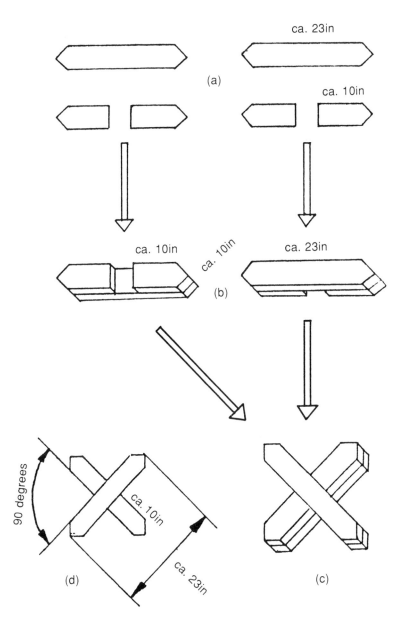

Figure 59. For construction of the cavalletti described here:
a) the 2 long and 4 short side pieces; b) long and short pieces
are joined (see also Fig. 60, 61); c) the finished cross;
d) dimensions.

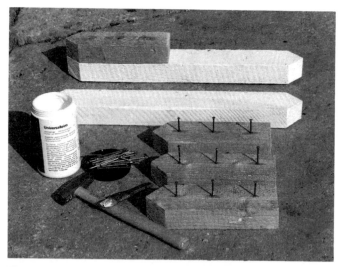

Figure 60.

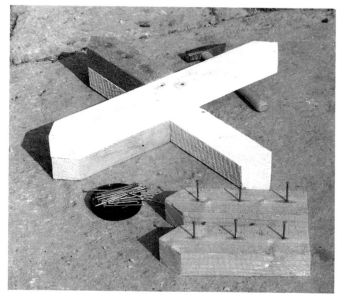

Figure 61.

of the long side pieces (Fig. 62). All of this makes the cavalletti especially stable.

The dimensions are shown in Figure 59d. The bars of the crosses are about 4in (10cm) thick, and short—they don't stick up very far. The most important thing about these measurements is that they minimize the risk of injury.

The perfect fit of the crosses on either end

Figure 62. Boring holes for nailing the pole to the cross.

Figure 63. The good fit of this cavalletti proves useful for setting up jumps.

ensures that two or more cavalletti stacked on top of each other will remain stable even if they are lightly knocked against. This fit also makes it easy to erect uprights and oxers (Fig. 63).

If the cavalletti are intended for use in smaller competitions, their round wooden poles must be 13.2ft (4m) long. At least six cavalletti are needed for the basic stages of training, more for advanced work.

Index

Agility of horse, 60

Back injuries, 90
  and convalescing horses,
    70
Balance, 4, 22, 27, 31, 43,
    64, 72

Calm, importance of, 24, 34,
    49
Caprilli, Federico, 2
Cavalletti
  importance of distances,
    13, 39
  spacing of, 15
Center of gravity, 28, 42, 63
Centrifugal force, 60
Concours Hippique Interna-
    tional Officiel, 5
Correction, while moving, 20
Course of instruction, diversi-
    fication of, 42
Cross-country hacking, 109
  jumps, 36
  work, 86

De Nemethy, Bertalan, 2
Demands of modern jumping
  competition, 83

Establishment of trust, 101

Forward motion of trot, 27
Forward riding, 2
Forward seat, jumping, 51,
    81
Forward-driving aids, and
    timing, 114

Gymnastic exercise, 2, 24,
    32,

Hands, give of, 17, 19, 21,
    28, 31, 35, 48, 109
Honest jumps, 73, 119
Horse
  accurate movements, 4
  bend of, 56, 61
  consideration for, 32
  increased concentration, 4
  injuries to legs, 12, 16, 84
  mistreatment of, 6
  possible injuries to, 38
  reducing stress of, 24, 83,
    118
  and rider, balance and
    equilibrium, 90
  and rider, trust between,
    5, 31, 65, 117

Horse (cont.)
    rider's coordination with,
       31
    sense of security and self-
       confidence, 25, 73
    warming up, 19
Increase of challenge
    and jumping, 4, 77
    and timing, 64
Individual needs, formations
    for, 75

Jumping, slow-motion version
    of, 4, 30
Jumps
    approach to, 108
    size of in schooling, 85

Lactic acid, buildup of, 85
Leg aids, 97
Length of stride, 56
Lerch, Volker, 128
Level of instruction, individual
    evaluation of, 8
Light seat, 22

Movement, natural coordina-
    tion of, 43

Natural Method, 1

Patience, importance of, 44
Point of position, 19, 30, 35,
    49, 73, 109
Prerequisites for dressage
    horses, 95

Rein aids, 30, 35
Reins, release of, 26, 36
Restorative training, 86
Rhythm, self-determination
    of, 36
Rider, controlling influence of,
    52, 81
Riding aids, 17
Rising trot versus sitting trot,
    28

Schooling, 6
    individually adapted, 100
    progression of, 91
Seat aids, 30, 56, 72, 98,
    102, 108, 116
Side reins, use of, 89
Stirrups, shortened, 9
Supervision of qualified
    instructor, 43
Suspended phase, 23

Talking to horse, 19
Timing and rhythm, 23, 29,
    51, 68
Timing between competi-
    tions, 86
Training, patience in, 124
Trust, installation of, 84

Use of curves in training, 56

Veterinarian, discussion with,
    90
Vocal praise, use of, 10, 87,
    101, 118